MINDFULNESS JOURNAL

FOR TEEN BOYS

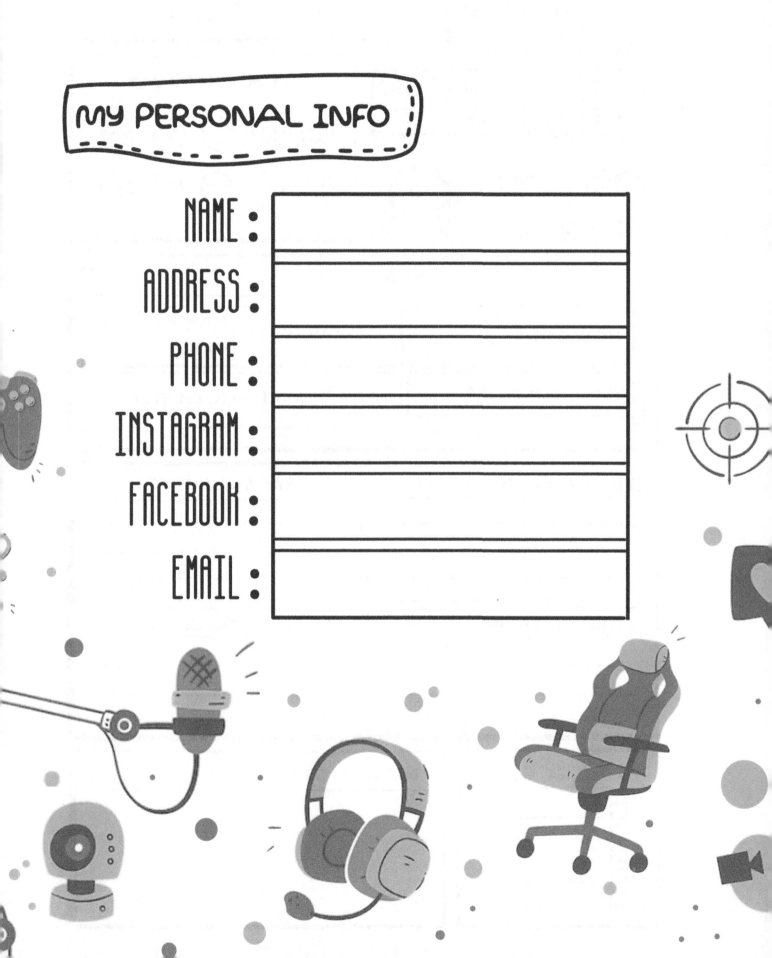

MY PERSONAL INFO

NAME :

ADDRESS :

PHONE :

INSTAGRAM :

FACEBOOK :

EMAIL :

MINDFULNESS DAILY JOURNAL

MON ☐ TUE ☐ WED ☐

THU ☐ FRI ☐ SAT ☐ SUN ☐

DATE: ____/____/20____

MY MOOD TODAY

MEDITATION

HOW LONG? ____/____

HOW WAS IT? HARD ☐ EASY ☐

EXCERCISE ☐

YOGA/WALKING/GYM/OTHER:
_____

✿ TODAY I CHOOSE TO FEEL
_____
_____
_____

⚲ TODAY I WILL FOCUS ON
_____
_____
_____

⚡ TODAY I FEEL INSPIRED BY
_____
_____
_____

🎲 GOOD HABITS OF THE DAY
_____
_____
_____

TO DO LIST
☐ _____
☐ _____
☐ _____
☐ _____
☐ _____

TODAY I'M GRATEFUL FOR

MINDFULNESS DAILY JOURNAL

10 MINUTES TO REFLECT ON YOUR DAY

3 MOMENTS YOU'D LIKE TO REMEMBER

ONE IDEA OF TODAY THAT YOU'D LIKE TO EXPLORE FURTHER

ONE OF THE DAY'S CHALLENGE BIG OR SMALL

WHAT I DID WRONG AND HOW TO AVOID THAT

MINDFULNESS DAILY JOURNAL

JOURNAL

_____

_____

_____

_____

_____

_____

_____

_____

_____

_____

_____

WOW

MINDFULNESS DAILY JOURNAL

MON ☐ TUE ☐ WED ☐

THU ☐ FRI ☐ SAT ☐ SUN ☐

DATE: ____/____/20___

MY MOOD TODAY

MEDITATION

HOW LONG? ___/___

HOW WAS IT? HARD ☐ EASY ☐

EXCERCISE ☐

YOGA/WALKING/GYM/OTHER:
_____

✦ TODAY I CHOOSE TO FEEL
_____
_____
_____

◉ TODAY I WILL FOCUS ON
_____
_____
_____

⚡ TODAY I FEEL INSPIRED BY
_____
_____
_____

🎲 GOOD HABITS OF THE DAY
_____
_____
_____

TO DO LIST 📝
☐ _____
☐ _____
☐ _____
☐ _____
☐ _____

TODAY I'M GRATEFUL FOR
_____

MINDFULNESS DAILY JOURNAL

MY DAY

10 MINUTES TO REFLECT ON YOUR DAY

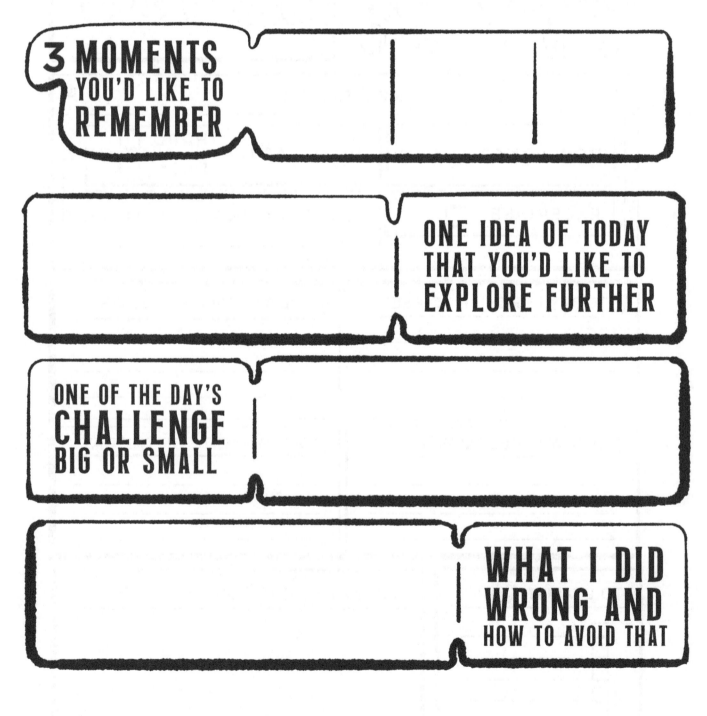

3 MOMENTS YOU'D LIKE TO **REMEMBER**

ONE IDEA OF TODAY THAT YOU'D LIKE TO EXPLORE FURTHER

ONE OF THE DAY'S CHALLENGE BIG OR SMALL

WHAT I DID WRONG AND HOW TO AVOID THAT

MINDFULNESS DAILY JOURNAL

JOURNAL

WOW

MINDFULNESS DAILY JOURNAL

MON ☐ **TUE** ☐ **WED** ☐

DATE: _____/_____/20___

THU ☐ **FRI** ☐ **SAT** ☐ **SUN** ☐

MY MOOD TODAY

MEDITATION

HOW LONG? ___/___

HOW WAS IT?   HARD ☐   EASY ☐

EXCERCISE ☐

YOGA/WALKING/GYM/OTHER:
_____

✴ TODAY I CHOOSE TO FEEL
_____
_____
_____
_____

◉ TODAY I WILL FOCUS ON
_____
_____
_____
_____

⚡ TODAY I FEEL INSPIRED BY
_____
_____
_____
_____

🎲 GOOD HABITS OF THE DAY
_____
_____
_____
_____

TO DO LIST 📝

☐ _____
☐ _____
☐ _____
☐ _____
☐ _____

TODAY I'M GRATEFUL FOR

MINDFULNESS DAILY JOURNAL

MY DAY

10 MINUTES TO REFLECT ON YOUR DAY

3 MOMENTS YOU'D LIKE TO REMEMBER

ONE IDEA OF TODAY THAT YOU'D LIKE TO EXPLORE FURTHER

ONE OF THE DAY'S CHALLENGE BIG OR SMALL

WHAT I DID WRONG AND HOW TO AVOID THAT

JOURNAL

_____

_____

_____

_____

_____

_____

_____

_____

_____

_____

_____

WOW

MINDFULNESS DAILY JOURNAL

MON ☐	TUE ☐	WED ☐
THU ☐	FRI ☐	SAT ☐	SUN ☐

DATE: _____ / _____ /20____

MY MOOD TODAY

MEDITATION

HOW LONG? _____ / _____

HOW WAS IT? **HARD** ☐ **EASY** ☐

EXCERCISE ☐

YOGA/WALKING/GYM/OTHER:
_____

✦ TODAY I CHOOSE TO FEEL
_____
_____
_____

◎ TODAY I WILL FOCUS ON
_____
_____
_____

⚡ TODAY I FEEL INSPIRED BY
_____
_____
_____

🎲 GOOD HABITS OF THE DAY
_____
_____
_____

TO DO LIST

☐ _____
☐ _____
☐ _____
☐ _____
☐ _____

TODAY I'M GRATEFUL FOR

MINDFULNESS DAILY JOURNAL

MY DAY

10 MINUTES TO REFLECT ON YOUR DAY

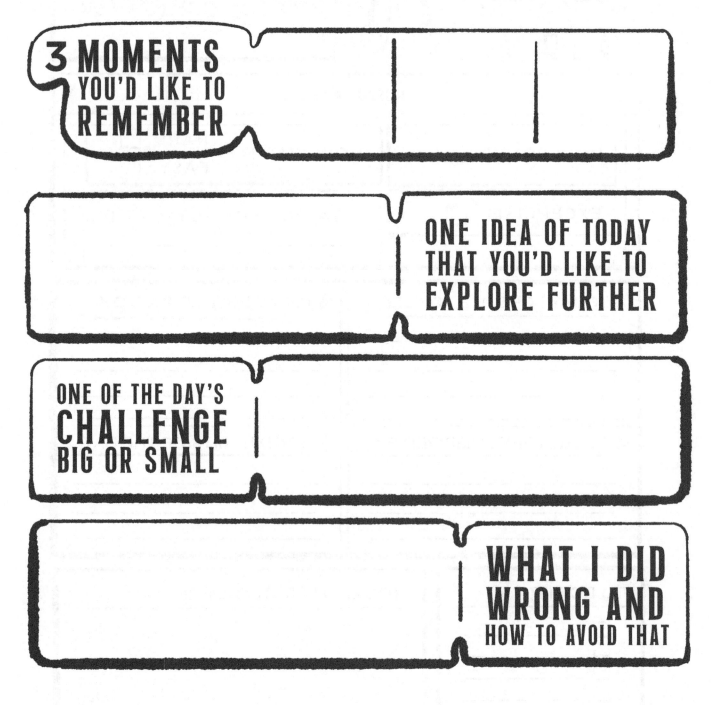

3 MOMENTS YOU'D LIKE TO REMEMBER

ONE IDEA OF TODAY THAT YOU'D LIKE TO EXPLORE FURTHER

ONE OF THE DAY'S CHALLENGE BIG OR SMALL

WHAT I DID WRONG AND HOW TO AVOID THAT

MINDFULNESS DAILY JOURNAL

JOURNAL

_____

_____

_____

_____

_____

_____

_____

_____

_____

_____

_____

WOW

MINDFULNESS DAILY JOURNAL

MON ☐	TUE ☐	WED ☐

THU ☐	FRI ☐	SAT ☐	SUN ☐

DATE: ____/____/20____

MY MOOD TODAY

MEDITATION

HOW LONG? ___/___

HOW WAS IT? HARD ☐ EASY ☐

EXCERCISE ☐

YOGA/WALKING/GYM/OTHER:
_____

✦ TODAY I CHOOSE TO FEEL
_____
_____
_____

◉ TODAY I WILL FOCUS ON
_____
_____
_____

⚡ TODAY I FEEL INSPIRED BY
_____
_____
_____

⚄ GOOD HABITS OF THE DAY
_____
_____
_____

TO DO LIST 📝
- ☐ _____
- ☐ _____
- ☐ _____
- ☐ _____
- ☐ _____

TODAY I'M GRATEFUL FOR

MINDFULNESS DAILY JOURNAL

10 MINUTES TO REFLECT ON YOUR DAY

3 MOMENTS YOU'D LIKE TO **REMEMBER**

ONE IDEA OF TODAY THAT YOU'D LIKE TO **EXPLORE FURTHER**

ONE OF THE DAY'S CHALLENGE BIG OR SMALL

WHAT I DID WRONG AND HOW TO AVOID THAT

MINDFULNESS DAILY JOURNAL

JOURNAL

WOW

MINDFULNESS DAILY JOURNAL

MON ☐	TUE ☐	WED ☐

DATE: ____/____/20____

THU ☐	FRI ☐	SAT ☐	SUN ☐

MY MOOD TODAY

MEDITATION

HOW LONG? ____/____

HOW WAS IT? HARD ☐ EASY ☐

EXCERCISE ☐

YOGA/WALKING/GYM/OTHER:
_____

✳ TODAY I CHOOSE TO FEEL
_____
_____
_____

◉ TODAY I WILL FOCUS ON
_____
_____
_____

⚡ TODAY I FEEL INSPIRED BY
_____
_____
_____

🎲 GOOD HABITS OF THE DAY
_____
_____
_____

TO DO LIST 📝

☐ _____
☐ _____
☐ _____
☐ _____
☐ _____

TODAY I'M GRATEFUL FOR

MINDFULNESS DAILY JOURNAL

MY DAY

10 MINUTES TO REFLECT ON YOUR DAY

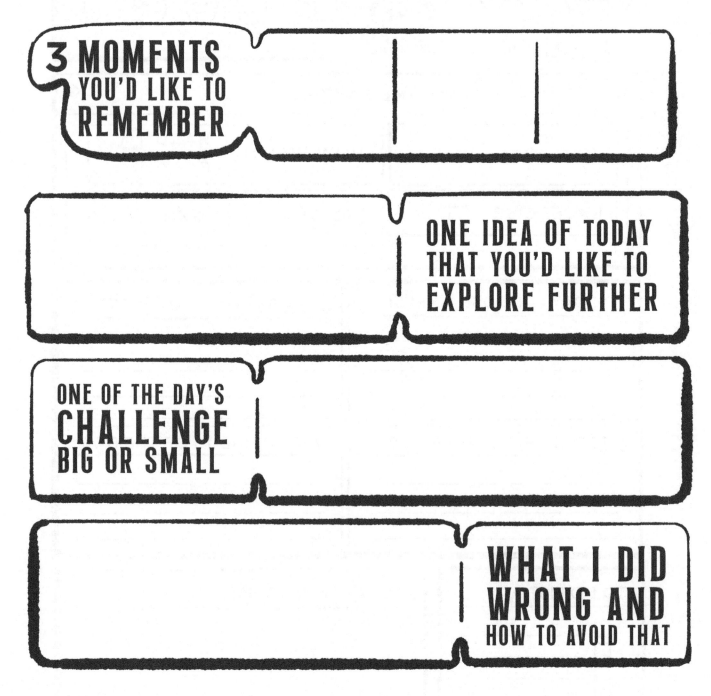

3 MOMENTS YOU'D LIKE TO **REMEMBER**

ONE IDEA OF TODAY THAT YOU'D LIKE TO EXPLORE FURTHER

ONE OF THE DAY'S CHALLENGE BIG OR SMALL

WHAT I DID WRONG AND HOW TO AVOID THAT

JOURNAL

_____

_____

_____

_____

_____

_____

_____

_____

_____

_____

_____

WOW

MINDFULNESS DAILY JOURNAL

MON ☐	TUE ☐	WED ☐

DATE: ____/____/20____

THU ☐	FRI ☐	SAT ☐	SUN ☐

MY MOOD TODAY

MEDITATION

HOW LONG? ___/___

HOW WAS IT?   HARD ☐   EASY ☐

EXCERCISE ☐

YOGA/WALKING/GYM/OTHER:
_____

✿ TODAY I CHOOSE TO FEEL
_____
_____
_____

◎ TODAY I WILL FOCUS ON
_____
_____
_____

⚡ TODAY I FEEL INSPIRED BY
_____
_____
_____

🎲 GOOD HABITS OF THE DAY
_____
_____
_____

TO DO LIST
☐ _____
☐ _____
☐ _____
☐ _____
☐ _____

TODAY I'M GRATEFUL FOR

MINDFULNESS DAILY JOURNAL

10 MINUTES TO REFLECT ON YOUR DAY

3 MOMENTS YOU'D LIKE TO REMEMBER

ONE IDEA OF TODAY THAT YOU'D LIKE TO EXPLORE FURTHER

ONE OF THE DAY'S CHALLENGE BIG OR SMALL

WHAT I DID WRONG AND HOW TO AVOID THAT

MINDFULNESS DAILY JOURNAL

JOURNAL

_____

_____

_____

_____

_____

_____

_____

_____

_____

_____

_____

WOW

MINDFULNESS DAILY JOURNAL

MON ☐	TUE ☐	WED ☐

THU ☐	FRI ☐	SAT ☐	SUN ☐

DATE: ____/____/20____

MY MOOD TODAY

MEDITATION

HOW LONG? ____/____

HOW WAS IT? HARD ☐   EASY ☐

EXCERCISE ☐

YOGA/WALKING/GYM/OTHER:
_____

✴ TODAY I CHOOSE TO FEEL
_____
_____
_____

◉ TODAY I WILL FOCUS ON
_____
_____
_____

⚡ TODAY I FEEL INSPIRED BY
_____
_____
_____

🎲 GOOD HABITS OF THE DAY
_____
_____
_____

TO DO LIST 📝
☐ _____
☐ _____
☐ _____
☐ _____
☐ _____

TODAY I'M GRATEFUL FOR

MINDFULNESS DAILY JOURNAL

MY DAY

10 MINUTES TO REFLECT ON YOUR DAY

3 MOMENTS YOU'D LIKE TO **REMEMBER**

ONE IDEA OF TODAY THAT YOU'D LIKE TO **EXPLORE FURTHER**

ONE OF THE DAY'S CHALLENGE BIG OR SMALL

WHAT I DID WRONG AND HOW TO AVOID THAT

MINDFULNESS DAILY JOURNAL

JOURNAL

WOW

MINDFULNESS DAILY JOURNAL

MON ☐ **TUE** ☐ **WED** ☐

THU ☐ **FRI** ☐ **SAT** ☐ **SUN** ☐

DATE: ____/____/20____

MY MOOD TODAY

MEDITATION

HOW LONG? ____/____

HOW WAS IT?   HARD ☐   EASY ☐

EXCERCISE ☐

YOGA/WALKING/GYM/OTHER:
_____

✴ TODAY I CHOOSE TO FEEL
_____
_____
_____

◉ TODAY I WILL FOCUS ON
_____
_____
_____

⚡ TODAY I FEEL INSPIRED BY
_____
_____
_____

🎲 GOOD HABITS OF THE DAY
_____
_____
_____

TO DO LIST 📝
☐ _____
☐ _____
☐ _____
☐ _____
☐ _____

TODAY I'M GRATEFUL FOR

MINDFULNESS DAILY JOURNAL

MY DAY

10 MINUTES TO REFLECT ON YOUR DAY

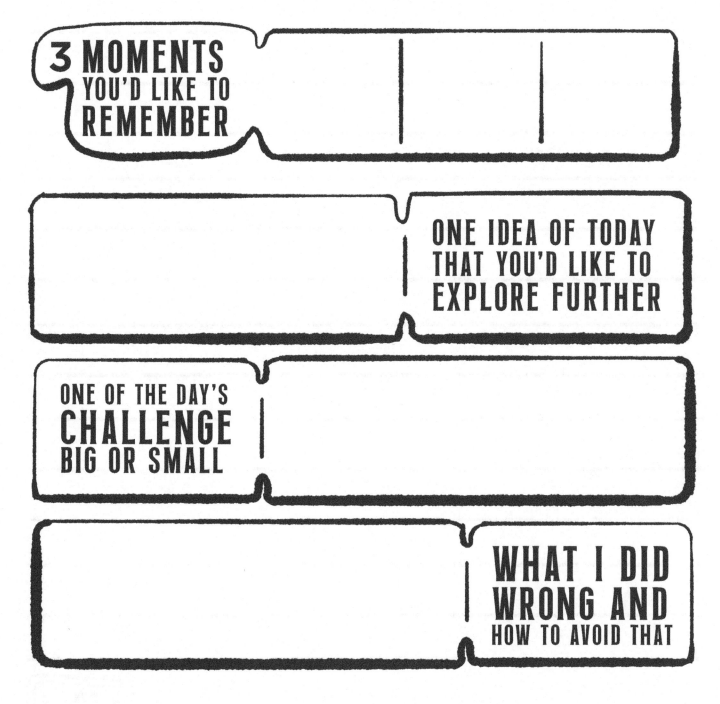

3 MOMENTS YOU'D LIKE TO REMEMBER

ONE IDEA OF TODAY THAT YOU'D LIKE TO EXPLORE FURTHER

ONE OF THE DAY'S CHALLENGE BIG OR SMALL

WHAT I DID WRONG AND HOW TO AVOID THAT

JOURNAL

WOW

MINDFULNESS DAILY JOURNAL

MON ☐ **TUE** ☐ **WED** ☐

DATE: ____ / ____ /20____

THU ☐ **FRI** ☐ **SAT** ☐ **SUN** ☐

MY MOOD TODAY

MEDITATION

HOW LONG? ____ / ____

HOW WAS IT? HARD ☐ EASY ☐

EXCERCISE ☐

YOGA/WALKING/GYM/OTHER:
_____

✦ TODAY I CHOOSE TO FEEL
_____
_____
_____

⊙ TODAY I WILL FOCUS ON
_____
_____
_____

⚡ TODAY I FEEL INSPIRED BY
_____
_____
_____

⚅ GOOD HABITS OF THE DAY
_____
_____
_____

TO DO LIST
☐ _____
☐ _____
☐ _____
☐ _____
☐ _____

TODAY I'M GRATEFUL FOR
_____

MINDFULNESS DAILY JOURNAL

MY DAY

10 MINUTES TO REFLECT ON YOUR DAY

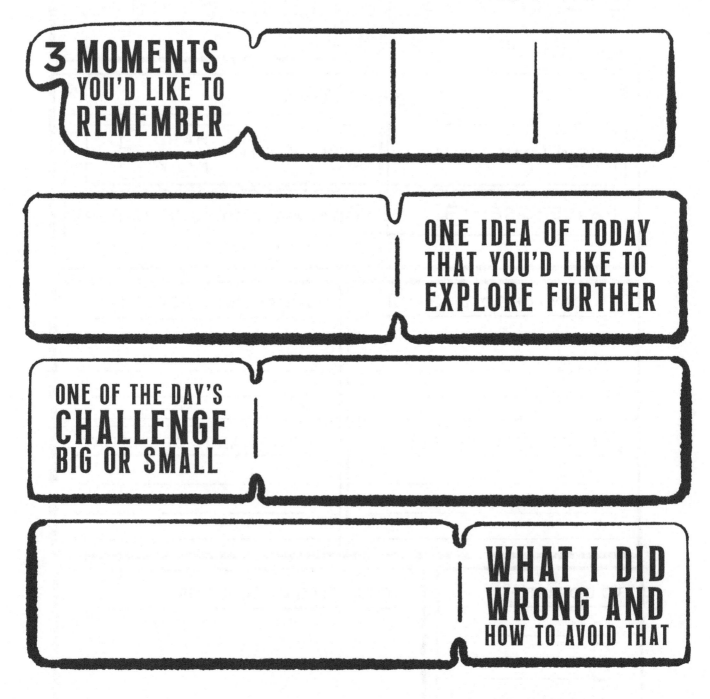

3 MOMENTS YOU'D LIKE TO REMEMBER

ONE IDEA OF TODAY THAT YOU'D LIKE TO EXPLORE FURTHER

ONE OF THE DAY'S CHALLENGE BIG OR SMALL

WHAT I DID WRONG AND HOW TO AVOID THAT

JOURNAL

MINDFULNESS DAILY JOURNAL

MON ☐	TUE ☐	WED ☐

THU ☐	FRI ☐	SAT ☐	SUN ☐

DATE: _____ / _____ / 20 _____

MY MOOD TODAY

MEDITATION

HOW LONG? ___/___

HOW WAS IT? HARD ☐ EASY ☐

EXCERCISE ☐

YOGA/WALKING/GYM/OTHER:
_____

✦ TODAY I CHOOSE TO FEEL
_____
_____
_____

⊙ TODAY I WILL FOCUS ON
_____
_____
_____

⚡ TODAY I FEEL INSPIRED BY
_____
_____
_____

⚂ GOOD HABITS OF THE DAY
_____
_____
_____

TO DO LIST 📝
☐ _____
☐ _____
☐ _____
☐ _____
☐ _____

TODAY I'M GRATEFUL FOR
_____

MINDFULNESS DAILY JOURNAL

MY DAY

10 MINUTES TO REFLECT ON YOUR DAY

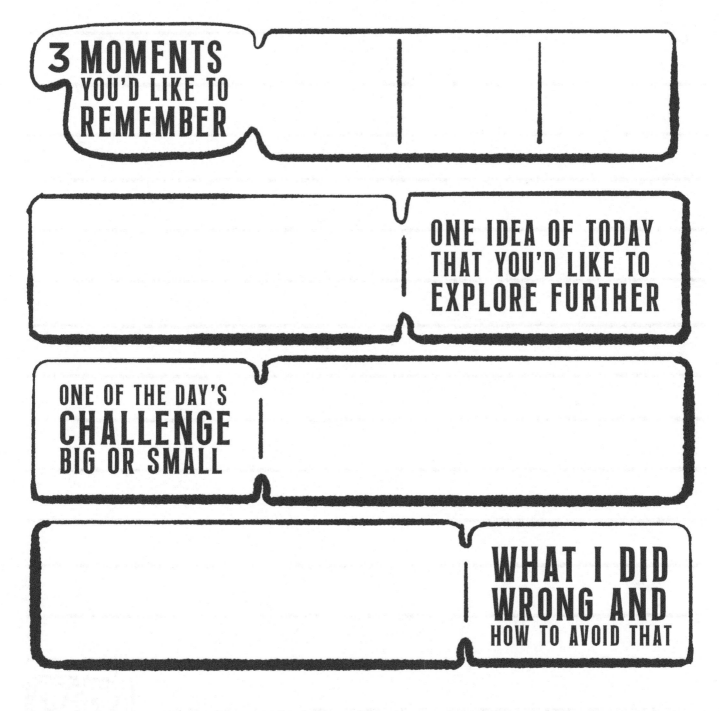

3 MOMENTS YOU'D LIKE TO REMEMBER

ONE IDEA OF TODAY THAT YOU'D LIKE TO EXPLORE FURTHER

ONE OF THE DAY'S CHALLENGE BIG OR SMALL

WHAT I DID WRONG AND HOW TO AVOID THAT

MINDFULNESS DAILY JOURNAL

JOURNAL

_____

_____

_____

_____

_____

_____

_____

_____

_____

_____

_____

_____

WOW

MINDFULNESS DAILY JOURNAL

MON ☐	TUE ☐	WED ☐

THU ☐	FRI ☐	SAT ☐	SUN ☐

DATE: ____/____/20____

MY MOOD TODAY

MEDITATION

HOW LONG? ____/____

HOW WAS IT? HARD ☐ EASY ☐

EXCERCISE ☐

YOGA/WALKING/GYM/OTHER:
_____

✦ TODAY I CHOOSE TO FEEL
_____
_____
_____
_____

◉ TODAY I WILL FOCUS ON
_____
_____
_____
_____

⚡ TODAY I FEEL INSPIRED BY
_____
_____
_____
_____

🎲 GOOD HABITS OF THE DAY
_____
_____
_____
_____

TO DO LIST 📝
☐ _____
☐ _____
☐ _____
☐ _____
☐ _____

TODAY I'M GRATEFUL FOR

MINDFULNESS DAILY JOURNAL

10 MINUTES TO REFLECT ON YOUR DAY

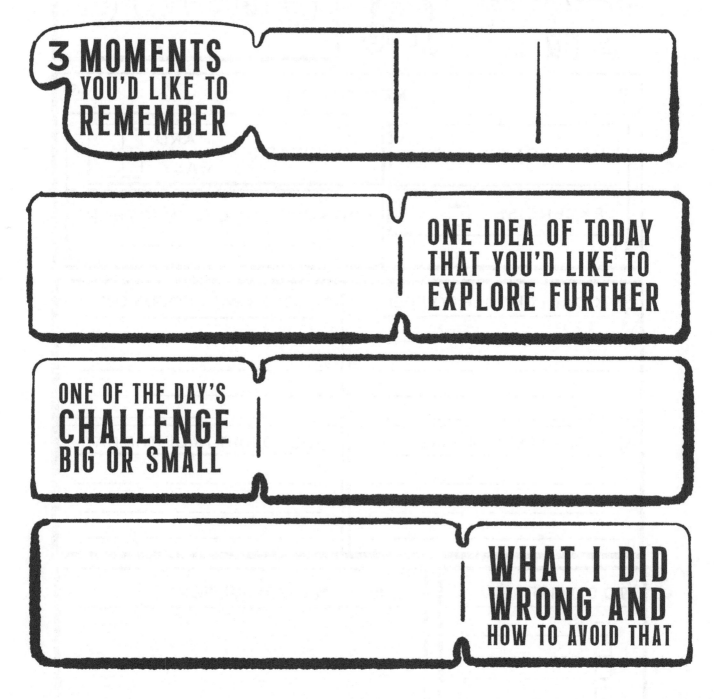

3 MOMENTS YOU'D LIKE TO REMEMBER

ONE IDEA OF TODAY THAT YOU'D LIKE TO EXPLORE FURTHER

ONE OF THE DAY'S CHALLENGE BIG OR SMALL

WHAT I DID WRONG AND HOW TO AVOID THAT

MINDFULNESS DAILY JOURNAL

JOURNAL

```
_____
_____
_____
_____
_____
_____
_____
_____
_____
_____
_____
```

WOW

MINDFULNESS DAILY JOURNAL

MON ☐ TUE ☐ WED ☐

DATE: ____/____/20____

THU ☐ FRI ☐ SAT ☐ SUN ☐

MY MOOD TODAY

MEDITATION

HOW LONG? ____/____

HOW WAS IT? HARD ☐ EASY ☐

EXCERCISE ☐

YOGA/WALKING/GYM/OTHER:
_____

✺ TODAY I CHOOSE TO FEEL
_____
_____
_____

⊙ TODAY I WILL FOCUS ON
_____
_____
_____

⚡ TODAY I FEEL INSPIRED BY
_____
_____
_____

🎲 GOOD HABITS OF THE DAY
_____
_____
_____

TO DO LIST
☐ _____
☐ _____
☐ _____
☐ _____
☐ _____

TODAY I'M GRATEFUL FOR

MINDFULNESS DAILY JOURNAL

MY DAY

10 MINUTES TO REFLECT ON YOUR DAY

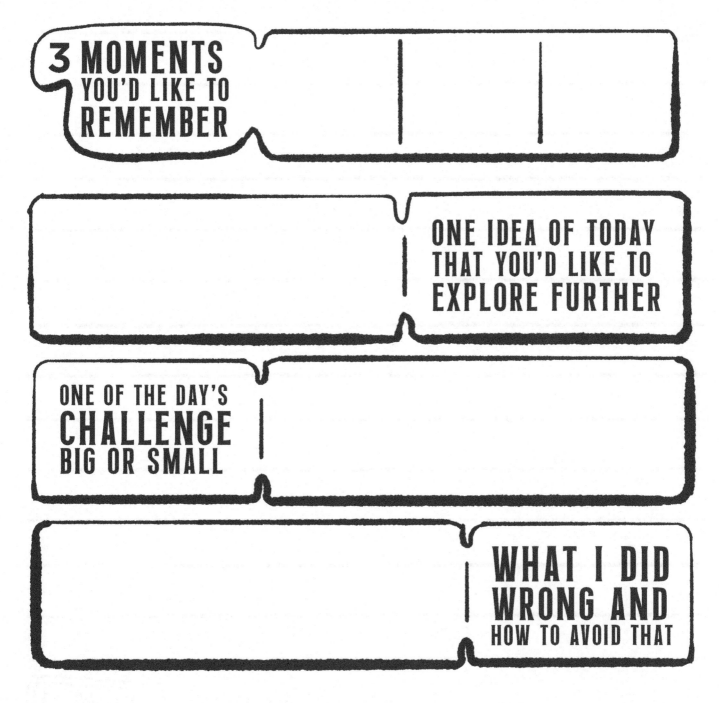

3 MOMENTS YOU'D LIKE TO REMEMBER

ONE IDEA OF TODAY THAT YOU'D LIKE TO EXPLORE FURTHER

ONE OF THE DAY'S CHALLENGE BIG OR SMALL

WHAT I DID WRONG AND HOW TO AVOID THAT

MINDFULNESS DAILY JOURNAL

JOURNAL

WOW

MINDFULNESS DAILY JOURNAL

MON ☐	TUE ☐	WED ☐

THU ☐	FRI ☐	SAT ☐	SUN ☐

DATE: ____/____/20____

MY MOOD TODAY

MEDITATION

HOW LONG? ____/____

HOW WAS IT? HARD ☐ EASY ☐

EXCERCISE ☐

YOGA/WALKING/GYM/OTHER:
_____

✸ TODAY I CHOOSE TO FEEL
_____
_____
_____

◉ TODAY I WILL FOCUS ON
_____
_____
_____

⚡ TODAY I FEEL INSPIRED BY
_____
_____
_____

🎲 GOOD HABITS OF THE DAY
_____
_____
_____

TO DO LIST 📝

☐ _____
☐ _____
☐ _____
☐ _____
☐ _____

TODAY I'M GRATEFUL FOR

MINDFULNESS DAILY JOURNAL

MY DAY

10 MINUTES TO REFLECT ON YOUR DAY

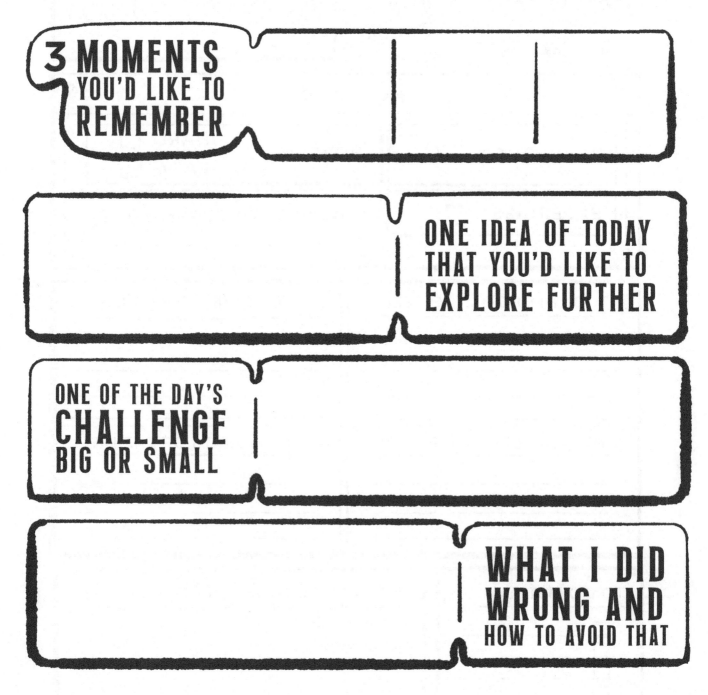

3 MOMENTS YOU'D LIKE TO REMEMBER

ONE IDEA OF TODAY THAT YOU'D LIKE TO EXPLORE FURTHER

ONE OF THE DAY'S CHALLENGE BIG OR SMALL

WHAT I DID WRONG AND HOW TO AVOID THAT

JOURNAL

WOW

MINDFULNESS DAILY JOURNAL

MON ☐　TUE ☐　WED ☐

THU ☐　FRI ☐　SAT ☐　SUN ☐

DATE: _____ / _____ /20_____

MY MOOD TODAY

MEDITATION

HOW LONG? _____ / _____

HOW WAS IT?　HARD ☐
　　　　　　　EASY ☐

EXCERCISE ☐

YOGA/WALKING/GYM/OTHER:
_____

✸ TODAY I CHOOSE TO FEEL
_____
_____
_____

◉ TODAY I WILL FOCUS ON
_____
_____
_____

⚡ TODAY I FEEL INSPIRED BY
_____
_____
_____

🎲 GOOD HABITS OF THE DAY
_____
_____
_____

TO DO LIST 📝
☐ _____
☐ _____
☐ _____
☐ _____
☐ _____

TODAY I'M GRATEFUL FOR

MINDFULNESS DAILY JOURNAL

MY DAY

10 MINUTES TO REFLECT ON YOUR DAY

3 MOMENTS YOU'D LIKE TO **REMEMBER**

ONE IDEA OF TODAY THAT YOU'D LIKE TO **EXPLORE FURTHER**

ONE OF THE DAY'S **CHALLENGE** BIG OR SMALL

WHAT I DID WRONG AND HOW TO AVOID THAT

JOURNAL

WOW

MINDFULNESS DAILY JOURNAL

MON ☐ **TUE** ☐ **WED** ☐

DATE: _____/_____/20_____

THU ☐ **FRI** ☐ **SAT** ☐ **SUN** ☐

MY MOOD TODAY

MEDITATION

HOW LONG? _____/_____

HOW WAS IT? HARD ☐ EASY ☐

EXCERCISE ☐

YOGA/WALKING/GYM/OTHER:
_____

✸ TODAY I CHOOSE TO FEEL
_____
_____
_____

⊙ TODAY I WILL FOCUS ON
_____
_____
_____

⚡ TODAY I FEEL INSPIRED BY
_____
_____
_____

⚅ GOOD HABITS OF THE DAY
_____
_____
_____

TO DO LIST 📝
☐ _____
☐ _____
☐ _____
☐ _____
☐ _____

TODAY I'M GRATEFUL FOR

MINDFULNESS DAILY JOURNAL

MY DAY

10 MINUTES TO REFLECT ON YOUR DAY

3 MOMENTS YOU'D LIKE TO REMEMBER

ONE IDEA OF TODAY THAT YOU'D LIKE TO EXPLORE FURTHER

ONE OF THE DAY'S CHALLENGE BIG OR SMALL

WHAT I DID WRONG AND HOW TO AVOID THAT

MINDFULNESS DAILY JOURNAL

JOURNAL

_____

_____

_____

_____

_____

_____

_____

_____

_____

_____

_____

WOW

MINDFULNESS DAILY JOURNAL

MON ☐	TUE ☐	WED ☐

DATE: ____/____/20___

THU ☐	FRI ☐	SAT ☐	SUN ☐

MY MOOD TODAY

MEDITATION

HOW LONG? ___/___

HOW WAS IT? HARD ☐ EASY ☐

EXCERCISE ☐

YOGA/WALKING/GYM/OTHER:
_____

✦ TODAY I CHOOSE TO FEEL
_____
_____
_____

◉ TODAY I WILL FOCUS ON
_____
_____
_____

⚡ TODAY I FEEL INSPIRED BY
_____
_____
_____

🎲 GOOD HABITS OF THE DAY
_____
_____
_____

TO DO LIST 📝
☐ _____
☐ _____
☐ _____
☐ _____
☐ _____

TODAY I'M GRATEFUL FOR
_____

MINDFULNESS DAILY JOURNAL

10 MINUTES TO REFLECT ON YOUR DAY

3 MOMENTS YOU'D LIKE TO REMEMBER

ONE IDEA OF TODAY THAT YOU'D LIKE TO EXPLORE FURTHER

ONE OF THE DAY'S CHALLENGE BIG OR SMALL

WHAT I DID WRONG AND HOW TO AVOID THAT

MINDFULNESS DAILY JOURNAL

JOURNAL

_____

_____

_____

_____

_____

_____

_____

_____

_____

_____

_____

WOW

MINDFULNESS DAILY JOURNAL

MON ☐ TUE ☐ WED ☐

THU ☐ FRI ☐ SAT ☐ SUN ☐

DATE: _____/_____/20_____

MY MOOD TODAY

MEDITATION

HOW LONG? _____/_____

HOW WAS IT? HARD ☐ EASY ☐

EXCERCISE ☐

YOGA/WALKING/GYM/OTHER:
_____

✦ TODAY I CHOOSE TO FEEL
_____
_____
_____

◉ TODAY I WILL FOCUS ON
_____
_____
_____

⚡ TODAY I FEEL INSPIRED BY
_____
_____
_____

🎲 GOOD HABITS OF THE DAY
_____
_____
_____

TO DO LIST 📝

☐ _____
☐ _____
☐ _____
☐ _____
☐ _____

TODAY I'M GRATEFUL FOR

MINDFULNESS DAILY JOURNAL

MY DAY

10 MINUTES TO REFLECT ON YOUR DAY

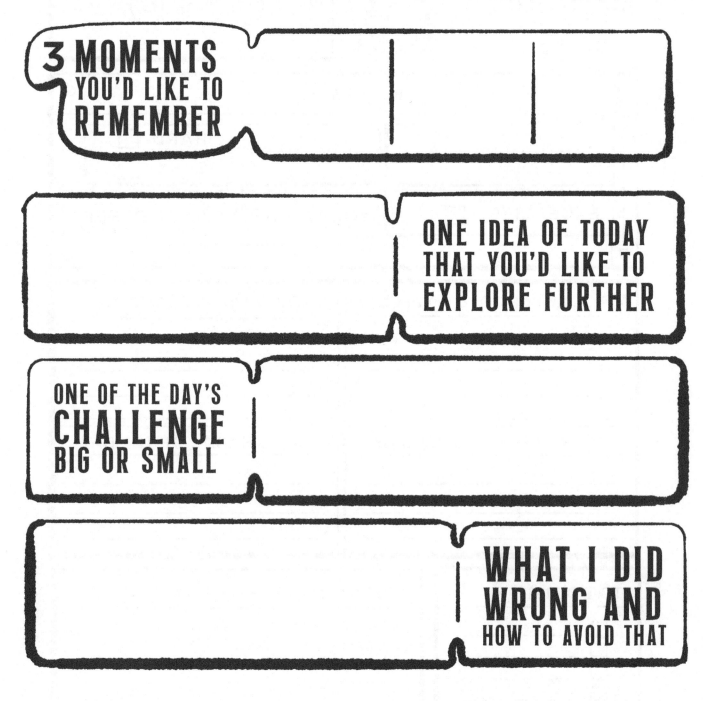

3 MOMENTS YOU'D LIKE TO REMEMBER

ONE IDEA OF TODAY THAT YOU'D LIKE TO EXPLORE FURTHER

ONE OF THE DAY'S CHALLENGE BIG OR SMALL

WHAT I DID WRONG AND HOW TO AVOID THAT

JOURNAL

_____

_____

_____

_____

_____

_____

_____

_____

_____

_____

_____

_____

_____

WOW

MINDFULNESS DAILY JOURNAL

MON ☐ TUE ☐ WED ☐

THU ☐ FRI ☐ SAT ☐ SUN ☐

DATE: _____/_____/20_____

MY MOOD TODAY

MEDITATION

HOW LONG? _____/_____

HOW WAS IT? HARD ☐ EASY ☐

EXCERCISE ☐

YOGA/WALKING/GYM/OTHER:
_____

✦ TODAY I CHOOSE TO FEEL
_____
_____
_____

◉ TODAY I WILL FOCUS ON
_____
_____
_____

⚡ TODAY I FEEL INSPIRED BY
_____
_____
_____

⚄ GOOD HABITS OF THE DAY
_____
_____
_____

TO DO LIST 📝

☐ _____
☐ _____
☐ _____
☐ _____
☐ _____

TODAY I'M GRATEFUL FOR

MINDFULNESS DAILY JOURNAL

MY DAY

10 MINUTES TO REFLECT ON YOUR DAY

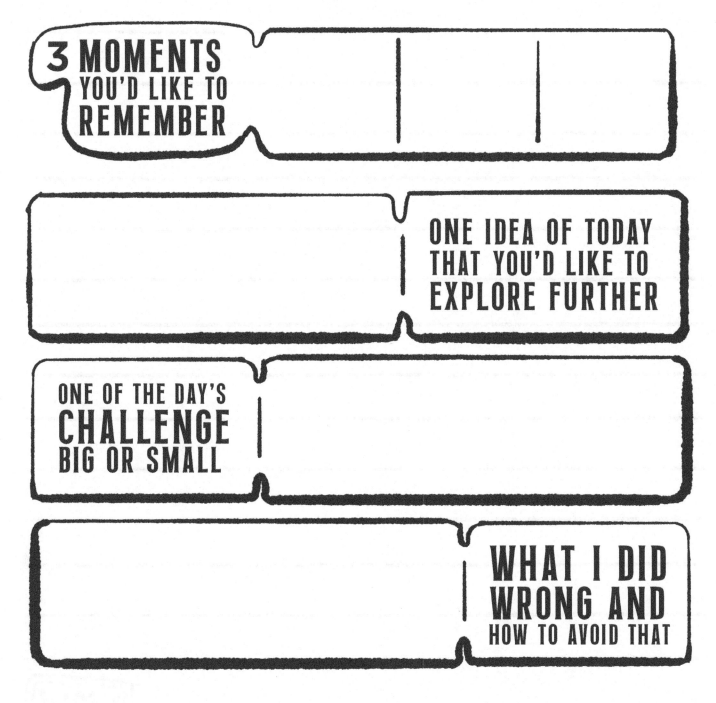

3 MOMENTS YOU'D LIKE TO REMEMBER

ONE IDEA OF TODAY THAT YOU'D LIKE TO EXPLORE FURTHER

ONE OF THE DAY'S CHALLENGE BIG OR SMALL

WHAT I DID WRONG AND HOW TO AVOID THAT

MINDFULNESS DAILY JOURNAL

JOURNAL

_____

_____

_____

_____

_____

_____

_____

_____

_____

_____

_____

WOW

MINDFULNESS DAILY JOURNAL

MON ☐   **TUE** ☐   **WED** ☐

THU ☐   **FRI** ☐   **SAT** ☐   **SUN** ☐

DATE: ____/____/20____

MY MOOD TODAY

MEDITATION

HOW LONG? ____/____

HOW WAS IT?   HARD ☐   EASY ☐

EXCERCISE ☐

YOGA/WALKING/GYM/OTHER:
_____

✦ TODAY I CHOOSE TO FEEL
_____
_____
_____

◉ TODAY I WILL FOCUS ON
_____
_____
_____

⚡ TODAY I FEEL INSPIRED BY
_____
_____
_____

⚅ GOOD HABITS OF THE DAY
_____
_____
_____

TO DO LIST 📝
☐ _____
☐ _____
☐ _____
☐ _____
☐ _____

TODAY I'M GRATEFUL FOR
_____

MINDFULNESS DAILY JOURNAL

MY DAY

10 MINUTES TO REFLECT ON YOUR DAY

3 MOMENTS YOU'D LIKE TO REMEMBER

ONE IDEA OF TODAY THAT YOU'D LIKE TO EXPLORE FURTHER

ONE OF THE DAY'S CHALLENGE BIG OR SMALL

WHAT I DID WRONG AND HOW TO AVOID THAT

MINDFULNESS DAILY JOURNAL

JOURNAL

_____

_____

_____

_____

_____

_____

_____

_____

_____

_____

_____

_____

WOW

MINDFULNESS DAILY JOURNAL

MON ☐	TUE ☐	WED ☐

DATE: ____ / ____ /20____

THU ☐	FRI ☐	SAT ☐	SUN ☐

MY MOOD TODAY

MEDITATION

HOW LONG? ____ / ____

HOW WAS IT? HARD ☐ EASY ☐

EXCERCISE ☐

YOGA/WALKING/GYM/OTHER:
_____

✳ TODAY I CHOOSE TO FEEL
_____
_____
_____

◉ TODAY I WILL FOCUS ON
_____
_____
_____

⚡ TODAY I FEEL INSPIRED BY
_____
_____
_____

🎲 GOOD HABITS OF THE DAY
_____
_____
_____

TO DO LIST 📝
- ☐ _____
- ☐ _____
- ☐ _____
- ☐ _____
- ☐ _____

TODAY I'M GRATEFUL FOR

MINDFULNESS DAILY JOURNAL

MY DAY

10 MINUTES TO REFLECT ON YOUR DAY

3 MOMENTS YOU'D LIKE TO REMEMBER

ONE IDEA OF TODAY THAT YOU'D LIKE TO EXPLORE FURTHER

ONE OF THE DAY'S CHALLENGE BIG OR SMALL

WHAT I DID WRONG AND HOW TO AVOID THAT

MINDFULNESS DAILY JOURNAL

JOURNAL

WOW

MINDFULNESS DAILY JOURNAL

MON ☐ TUE ☐ WED ☐

THU ☐ FRI ☐ SAT ☐ SUN ☐

DATE: _____/_____/20_____

MY MOOD TODAY

MEDITATION

HOW LONG? _____/_____

HOW WAS IT? HARD ☐ EASY ☐

EXCERCISE ☐

YOGA/WALKING/GYM/OTHER:
_____

✦ TODAY I CHOOSE TO FEEL
_____
_____
_____

◉ TODAY I WILL FOCUS ON
_____
_____
_____

⚡ TODAY I FEEL INSPIRED BY
_____
_____
_____

⚅ GOOD HABITS OF THE DAY
_____
_____
_____

TO DO LIST
☐ _____
☐ _____
☐ _____
☐ _____
☐ _____

TODAY I'M GRATEFUL FOR

MINDFULNESS DAILY JOURNAL

MY DAY

10 MINUTES TO REFLECT ON YOUR DAY

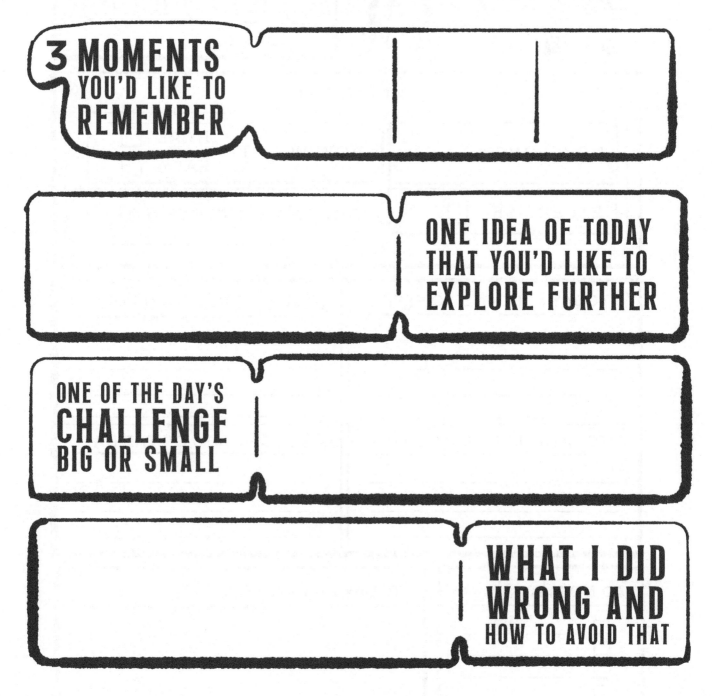

3 MOMENTS YOU'D LIKE TO REMEMBER

ONE IDEA OF TODAY THAT YOU'D LIKE TO EXPLORE FURTHER

ONE OF THE DAY'S CHALLENGE BIG OR SMALL

WHAT I DID WRONG AND HOW TO AVOID THAT

MINDFULNESS DAILY JOURNAL

JOURNAL

_____

_____

_____

_____

_____

_____

_____

_____

_____

_____

_____

_____

WOW

MINDFULNESS DAILY JOURNAL

MON ☐	TUE ☐	WED ☐

DATE: _____/_____/20____

THU ☐	FRI ☐	SAT ☐	SUN ☐

MY MOOD TODAY

MEDITATION

HOW LONG? ____/____

HOW WAS IT? HARD ☐ EASY ☐

EXCERCISE ☐

YOGA/WALKING/GYM/OTHER:
_____

✹ TODAY I CHOOSE TO FEEL
_____
_____
_____
_____

◉ TODAY I WILL FOCUS ON
_____
_____
_____
_____

⚡ TODAY I FEEL INSPIRED BY
_____
_____
_____
_____

🎲 GOOD HABITS OF THE DAY
_____
_____
_____
_____

TO DO LIST 📝

☐ _____
☐ _____
☐ _____
☐ _____
☐ _____

TODAY I'M GRATEFUL FOR

MINDFULNESS DAILY JOURNAL

10 MINUTES TO REFLECT ON YOUR DAY

3 MOMENTS YOU'D LIKE TO REMEMBER

ONE IDEA OF TODAY THAT YOU'D LIKE TO EXPLORE FURTHER

ONE OF THE DAY'S CHALLENGE BIG OR SMALL

WHAT I DID WRONG AND HOW TO AVOID THAT

MINDFULNESS DAILY JOURNAL

JOURNAL

WOW

MINDFULNESS DAILY JOURNAL

MON ☐	TUE ☐	WED ☐

DATE: ____/____/20___

THU ☐	FRI ☐	SAT ☐	SUN ☐

MY MOOD TODAY

MEDITATION

HOW LONG? ____/____

HOW WAS IT?　HARD ☐
　　　　　　　EASY ☐

EXCERCISE ☐

YOGA/WALKING/GYM/OTHER:
_____

✦ TODAY I CHOOSE TO FEEL
_____
_____
_____

◉ TODAY I WILL FOCUS ON
_____
_____
_____

⚡ TODAY I FEEL INSPIRED BY
_____
_____
_____

🎲 GOOD HABITS OF THE DAY
_____
_____
_____

TO DO LIST
- ☐ _____
- ☐ _____
- ☐ _____
- ☐ _____
- ☐ _____

TODAY I'M GRATEFUL FOR

MINDFULNESS DAILY JOURNAL

MY DAY

10 MINUTES TO REFLECT ON YOUR DAY

3 MOMENTS YOU'D LIKE TO REMEMBER

ONE IDEA OF TODAY THAT YOU'D LIKE TO EXPLORE FURTHER

ONE OF THE DAY'S CHALLENGE BIG OR SMALL

WHAT I DID WRONG AND HOW TO AVOID THAT

MINDFULNESS DAILY JOURNAL

JOURNAL

_____

_____

_____

_____

_____

_____

_____

_____

_____

_____

_____

_____

WOW

MINDFULNESS DAILY JOURNAL

MON	TUE	WED
☐	☐	☐

DATE: _____/_____/20____

THU	FRI	SAT	SUN
☐	☐	☐	☐

MY MOOD TODAY

MEDITATION

HOW LONG? ____/____

HOW WAS IT?   HARD ☐
EASY ☐

EXCERCISE ☐

YOGA/WALKING/GYM/OTHER:
_____

✤ TODAY I CHOOSE TO FEEL
_____
_____
_____

◉ TODAY I WILL FOCUS ON
_____
_____
_____

⚡ TODAY I FEEL INSPIRED BY
_____
_____
_____

🎲 GOOD HABITS OF THE DAY
_____
_____
_____

TO DO LIST 📝
☐ _____
☐ _____
☐ _____
☐ _____
☐ _____

TODAY I'M GRATEFUL FOR

MINDFULNESS DAILY JOURNAL

10 MINUTES TO REFLECT ON YOUR DAY

3 MOMENTS YOU'D LIKE TO REMEMBER

ONE IDEA OF TODAY THAT YOU'D LIKE TO EXPLORE FURTHER

ONE OF THE DAY'S CHALLENGE BIG OR SMALL

WHAT I DID WRONG AND HOW TO AVOID THAT

MINDFULNESS DAILY JOURNAL

JOURNAL

WOW

MINDFULNESS DAILY JOURNAL

MON ☐	TUE ☐	WED ☐

THU ☐	FRI ☐	SAT ☐	SUN ☐

DATE: ____/____/20____

MY MOOD TODAY

MEDITATION

HOW LONG? ____/____

HOW WAS IT?   HARD ☐   EASY ☐

EXCERCISE ☐

YOGA/WALKING/GYM/OTHER:
_____

✦ TODAY I CHOOSE TO FEEL
_____
_____
_____

◉ TODAY I WILL FOCUS ON
_____
_____
_____

⚡ TODAY I FEEL INSPIRED BY
_____
_____
_____

⚃ GOOD HABITS OF THE DAY
_____
_____
_____

TO DO LIST 📝
- ☐ _____
- ☐ _____
- ☐ _____
- ☐ _____
- ☐ _____

TODAY I'M GRATEFUL FOR
_____

MINDFULNESS DAILY JOURNAL

MY DAY

10 MINUTES TO REFLECT ON YOUR DAY

3 MOMENTS YOU'D LIKE TO REMEMBER

ONE IDEA OF TODAY THAT YOU'D LIKE TO EXPLORE FURTHER

ONE OF THE DAY'S CHALLENGE BIG OR SMALL

WHAT I DID WRONG AND HOW TO AVOID THAT

JOURNAL

WOW

MINDFULNESS DAILY JOURNAL

MON ☐   TUE ☐   WED ☐

THU ☐   FRI ☐   SAT ☐   SUN ☐

DATE: _____ / _____ /20 _____

MY MOOD TODAY

MEDITATION

HOW LONG? ___ / ___

HOW WAS IT?   HARD ☐   EASY ☐

EXCERCISE ☐

YOGA/WALKING/GYM/OTHER:
_____

⭐ TODAY I CHOOSE TO FEEL
_____
_____
_____

📍 TODAY I WILL FOCUS ON
_____
_____
_____

⚡ TODAY I FEEL INSPIRED BY
_____
_____
_____

🎲 GOOD HABITS OF THE DAY
_____
_____
_____

TO DO LIST
☐ _____
☐ _____
☐ _____
☐ _____
☐ _____

TODAY I'M GRATEFUL FOR

MINDFULNESS DAILY JOURNAL

MY DAY

10 MINUTES TO REFLECT ON YOUR DAY

3 MOMENTS YOU'D LIKE TO REMEMBER

ONE IDEA OF TODAY THAT YOU'D LIKE TO EXPLORE FURTHER

ONE OF THE DAY'S CHALLENGE BIG OR SMALL

WHAT I DID WRONG AND HOW TO AVOID THAT

MINDFULNESS DAILY JOURNAL

JOURNAL

WOW

MINDFULNESS DAILY JOURNAL

MON ☐	TUE ☐	WED ☐

DATE: _____/_____/20____

THU ☐	FRI ☐	SAT ☐	SUN ☐

MY MOOD TODAY

MEDITATION

HOW LONG? ____/____

HOW WAS IT? HARD ☐ EASY ☐

EXCERCISE ☐

YOGA/WALKING/GYM/OTHER:
_____

✦ TODAY I CHOOSE TO FEEL
_____
_____
_____

◉ TODAY I WILL FOCUS ON
_____
_____
_____

⚡ TODAY I FEEL INSPIRED BY
_____
_____
_____

⚅ GOOD HABITS OF THE DAY
_____
_____
_____

TO DO LIST 📝

☐ _____
☐ _____
☐ _____
☐ _____
☐ _____

TODAY I'M GRATEFUL FOR

MINDFULNESS DAILY JOURNAL

MY DAY

10 MINUTES TO REFLECT ON YOUR DAY

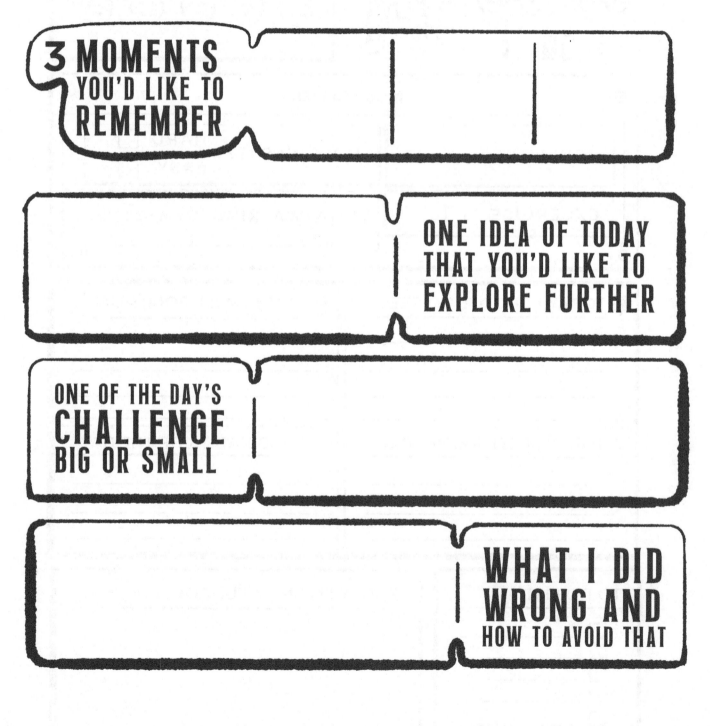

3 MOMENTS YOU'D LIKE TO **REMEMBER**

ONE IDEA OF TODAY THAT YOU'D LIKE TO **EXPLORE FURTHER**

ONE OF THE DAY'S CHALLENGE BIG OR SMALL

WHAT I DID WRONG AND HOW TO AVOID THAT

JOURNAL

_____

_____

_____

_____

_____

_____

_____

_____

_____

_____

_____

_____

WOW

MINDFULNESS DAILY JOURNAL

MON ☐ TUE ☐ WED ☐

THU ☐ FRI ☐ SAT ☐ SUN ☐

DATE: ____ / ____ /20____

MY MOOD TODAY

MEDITATION

HOW LONG? ___/___

HOW WAS IT? HARD ☐ EASY ☐

EXCERCISE ☐

YOGA/WALKING/GYM/OTHER:
_____

✦ TODAY I CHOOSE TO FEEL
_____
_____
_____

◉ TODAY I WILL FOCUS ON
_____
_____
_____

⚡ TODAY I FEEL INSPIRED BY
_____
_____
_____

🎲 GOOD HABITS OF THE DAY
_____
_____
_____

TO DO LIST
☐ _____
☐ _____
☐ _____
☐ _____
☐ _____

TODAY I'M GRATEFUL FOR

MINDFULNESS DAILY JOURNAL

MY DAY

10 MINUTES TO REFLECT ON YOUR DAY

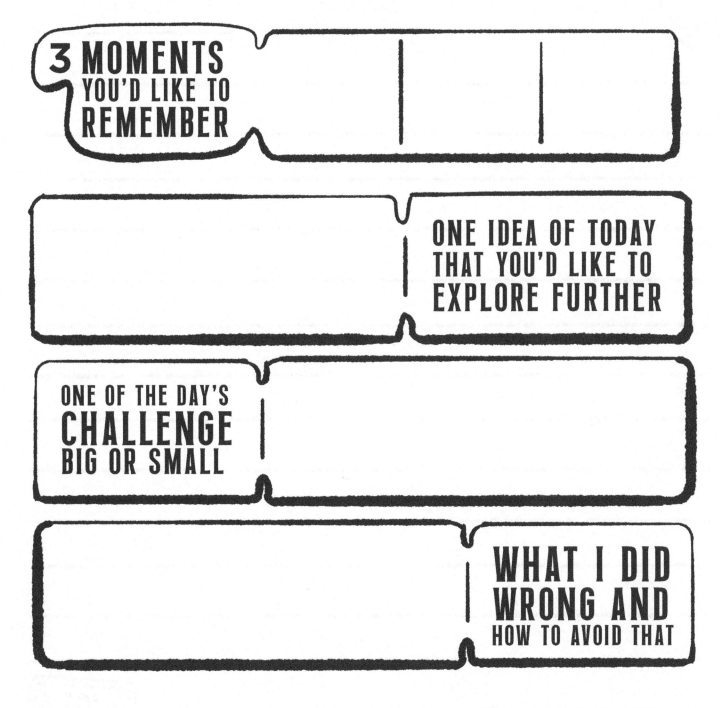

3 MOMENTS YOU'D LIKE TO **REMEMBER**

ONE IDEA OF TODAY THAT YOU'D LIKE TO EXPLORE FURTHER

ONE OF THE DAY'S CHALLENGE BIG OR SMALL

WHAT I DID WRONG AND HOW TO AVOID THAT

MINDFULNESS DAILY JOURNAL

JOURNAL

WOW

MINDFULNESS DAILY JOURNAL

MON ☐ **TUE** ☐ **WED** ☐

DATE: ____/____/20____

THU ☐ **FRI** ☐ **SAT** ☐ **SUN** ☐

MY MOOD TODAY

MEDITATION

HOW LONG? ____/____

HOW WAS IT? HARD ☐ EASY ☐

EXCERCISE ☐

YOGA/WALKING/GYM/OTHER:
_____

✦ TODAY I CHOOSE TO FEEL
_____
_____
_____

⚲ TODAY I WILL FOCUS ON
_____
_____
_____

⚡ TODAY I FEEL INSPIRED BY
_____
_____
_____

⚅ GOOD HABITS OF THE DAY
_____
_____
_____

TO DO LIST 📝

☐ _____
☐ _____
☐ _____
☐ _____
☐ _____

TODAY I'M GRATEFUL FOR
_____

MINDFULNESS DAILY JOURNAL

MY DAY

10 MINUTES TO REFLECT ON YOUR DAY

3 MOMENTS YOU'D LIKE TO REMEMBER

ONE IDEA OF TODAY THAT YOU'D LIKE TO EXPLORE FURTHER

ONE OF THE DAY'S CHALLENGE BIG OR SMALL

WHAT I DID WRONG AND HOW TO AVOID THAT

MINDFULNESS DAILY JOURNAL

JOURNAL

WOW

MINDFULNESS DAILY JOURNAL

MON ☐	TUE ☐	WED ☐

DATE: ____/____/20____

THU ☐	FRI ☐	SAT ☐	SUN ☐

MY MOOD TODAY

MEDITATION

HOW LONG? ____/____

HOW WAS IT?   HARD ☐   EASY ☐

EXCERCISE ☐

YOGA/WALKING/GYM/OTHER:
_____

❋ TODAY I CHOOSE TO FEEL
_____
_____
_____

◉ TODAY I WILL FOCUS ON
_____
_____
_____

⚡ TODAY I FEEL INSPIRED BY
_____
_____
_____

⚅ GOOD HABITS OF THE DAY
_____
_____
_____

TO DO LIST
☐ _____
☐ _____
☐ _____
☐ _____
☐ _____

TODAY I'M GRATEFUL FOR

MINDFULNESS DAILY JOURNAL

10 MINUTES TO REFLECT ON YOUR DAY

3 MOMENTS YOU'D LIKE TO REMEMBER

ONE IDEA OF TODAY THAT YOU'D LIKE TO EXPLORE FURTHER

ONE OF THE DAY'S CHALLENGE BIG OR SMALL

WHAT I DID WRONG AND HOW TO AVOID THAT

MINDFULNESS DAILY JOURNAL

JOURNAL

> 💬 _____

_____

_____

_____

_____

_____

_____

_____

_____

_____

_____

_____

_____ WOW

MINDFULNESS DAILY JOURNAL

MON ☐ TUE ☐ WED ☐

THU ☐ FRI ☐ SAT ☐ SUN ☐

DATE: ____/____/20___

MY MOOD TODAY

MEDITATION

HOW LONG? ___/___

HOW WAS IT? HARD ☐ EASY ☐

EXCERCISE ☐

YOGA/WALKING/GYM/OTHER:
_____

☆ TODAY I CHOOSE TO FEEL
_____
_____
_____

⚲ TODAY I WILL FOCUS ON
_____
_____
_____

⚡ TODAY I FEEL INSPIRED BY
_____
_____
_____

⚃ GOOD HABITS OF THE DAY
_____
_____
_____

TO DO LIST 📝
☐ _____
☐ _____
☐ _____
☐ _____
☐ _____

TODAY I'M GRATEFUL FOR
_____

MINDFULNESS DAILY JOURNAL

MY DAY

10 MINUTES TO REFLECT ON YOUR DAY

3 MOMENTS YOU'D LIKE TO REMEMBER

ONE IDEA OF TODAY THAT YOU'D LIKE TO EXPLORE FURTHER

ONE OF THE DAY'S CHALLENGE BIG OR SMALL

WHAT I DID WRONG AND HOW TO AVOID THAT

MINDFULNESS DAILY JOURNAL

JOURNAL

WOW

MINDFULNESS DAILY JOURNAL

MON	TUE	WED
☐	☐	☐

DATE: _____/_____/20_____

THU	FRI	SAT	SUN
☐	☐	☐	☐

MY MOOD TODAY

MEDITATION

HOW LONG? _____/_____

HOW WAS IT? HARD ☐ EASY ☐

EXCERCISE ☐

YOGA/WALKING/GYM/OTHER:
_____

✦ TODAY I CHOOSE TO FEEL
_____
_____
_____

◎ TODAY I WILL FOCUS ON
_____
_____
_____

⚡ TODAY I FEEL INSPIRED BY
_____
_____
_____

🎲 GOOD HABITS OF THE DAY
_____
_____
_____

TO DO LIST
☐ _____
☐ _____
☐ _____
☐ _____
☐ _____

TODAY I'M GRATEFUL FOR

MINDFULNESS DAILY JOURNAL

MY DAY

10 MINUTES TO REFLECT ON YOUR DAY

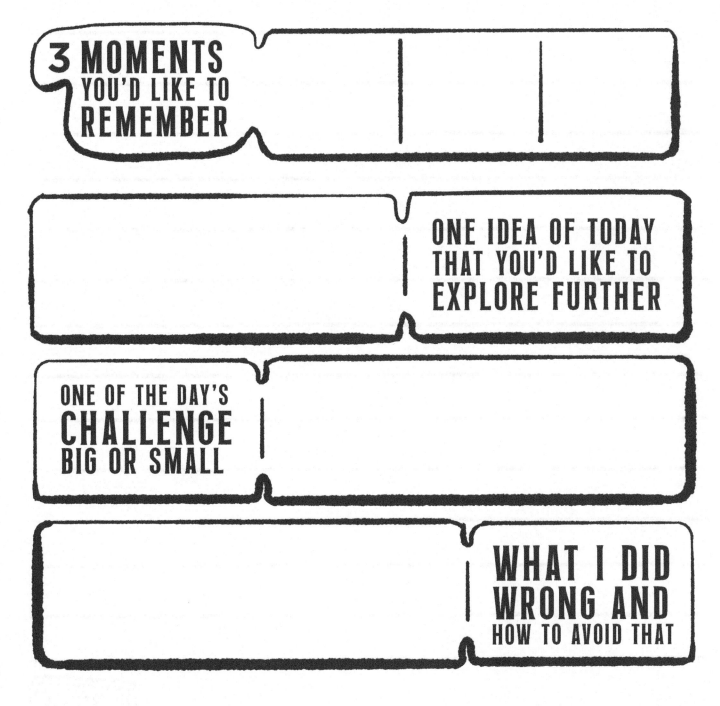

3 MOMENTS YOU'D LIKE TO REMEMBER

ONE IDEA OF TODAY THAT YOU'D LIKE TO EXPLORE FURTHER

ONE OF THE DAY'S CHALLENGE BIG OR SMALL

WHAT I DID WRONG AND HOW TO AVOID THAT

MINDFULNESS DAILY JOURNAL

JOURNAL

WOW

MINDFULNESS DAILY JOURNAL

MON	TUE	WED
☐	☐	☐

DATE: _____/_____/20_____

THU	FRI	SAT	SUN
☐	☐	☐	☐

MY MOOD TODAY

MEDITATION

HOW LONG? _____/_____

HOW WAS IT? HARD ☐ EASY ☐

EXCERCISE ☐

YOGA/WALKING/GYM/OTHER:
_____

✵ TODAY I CHOOSE TO FEEL
_____
_____
_____

⌖ TODAY I WILL FOCUS ON
_____
_____
_____

⚡ TODAY I FEEL INSPIRED BY
_____
_____
_____

⚄ GOOD HABITS OF THE DAY
_____
_____
_____

TO DO LIST 📝
☐ _____
☐ _____
☐ _____
☐ _____
☐ _____

TODAY I'M GRATEFUL FOR

MINDFULNESS DAILY JOURNAL

MY DAY

10 MINUTES TO REFLECT ON YOUR DAY

3 MOMENTS YOU'D LIKE TO REMEMBER

ONE IDEA OF TODAY THAT YOU'D LIKE TO EXPLORE FURTHER

ONE OF THE DAY'S CHALLENGE BIG OR SMALL

WHAT I DID WRONG AND HOW TO AVOID THAT

MINDFULNESS DAILY JOURNAL

JOURNAL

WOW

MINDFULNESS DAILY JOURNAL

MON ☐	TUE ☐	WED ☐

DATE: ____/____/20____

THU ☐	FRI ☐	SAT ☐	SUN ☐

MY MOOD TODAY

MEDITATION

HOW LONG? ____/____

HOW WAS IT? HARD ☐ EASY ☐

EXCERCISE ☐

YOGA/WALKING/GYM/OTHER:
_____

✦ TODAY I CHOOSE TO FEEL
_____
_____
_____
_____

◉ TODAY I WILL FOCUS ON
_____
_____
_____
_____

⚡ TODAY I FEEL INSPIRED BY
_____
_____
_____
_____

⚅ GOOD HABITS OF THE DAY
_____
_____
_____
_____

TO DO LIST 📝
☐ _____
☐ _____
☐ _____
☐ _____
☐ _____

TODAY I'M GRATEFUL FOR
_____

MINDFULNESS DAILY JOURNAL

MY DAY

10 MINUTES TO REFLECT ON YOUR DAY

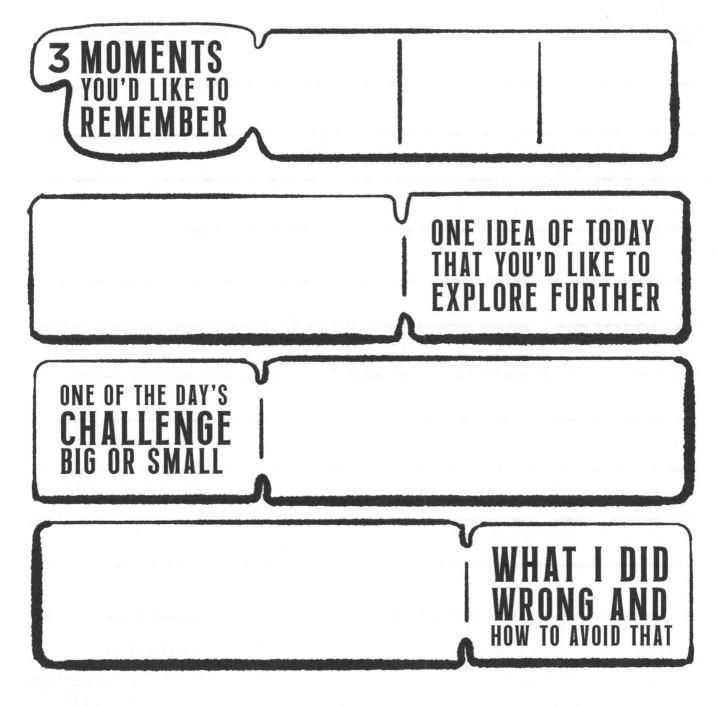

3 MOMENTS YOU'D LIKE TO REMEMBER

ONE IDEA OF TODAY THAT YOU'D LIKE TO EXPLORE FURTHER

ONE OF THE DAY'S CHALLENGE BIG OR SMALL

WHAT I DID WRONG AND HOW TO AVOID THAT

MINDFULNESS DAILY JOURNAL

JOURNAL

_____

_____

_____

_____

_____

_____

_____

_____

_____

_____

_____

WOW

MINDFULNESS DAILY JOURNAL

MON ☐	TUE ☐	WED ☐

DATE: ____/____/20____

THU ☐	FRI ☐	SAT ☐	SUN ☐

MY MOOD TODAY

MEDITATION

HOW LONG? ____/____

HOW WAS IT? HARD ☐ EASY ☐

EXCERCISE ☐

YOGA/WALKING/GYM/OTHER:
_____

✳ TODAY I CHOOSE TO FEEL
_____
_____
_____

◉ TODAY I WILL FOCUS ON
_____
_____
_____

⚡ TODAY I FEEL INSPIRED BY
_____
_____
_____

🎲 GOOD HABITS OF THE DAY
_____
_____
_____

TO DO LIST
- ☐ _____
- ☐ _____
- ☐ _____
- ☐ _____
- ☐ _____

TODAY I'M GRATEFUL FOR

MINDFULNESS DAILY JOURNAL

MY DAY

10 MINUTES TO REFLECT ON YOUR DAY

3 MOMENTS YOU'D LIKE TO REMEMBER

ONE IDEA OF TODAY THAT YOU'D LIKE TO EXPLORE FURTHER

ONE OF THE DAY'S CHALLENGE BIG OR SMALL

WHAT I DID WRONG AND HOW TO AVOID THAT

JOURNAL

_____

_____

_____

_____

_____

_____

_____

_____

_____

_____

_____

WOW

MINDFULNESS DAILY JOURNAL

MON ☐	TUE ☐	WED ☐

DATE: _____ / _____ / 20_____

THU ☐	FRI ☐	SAT ☐	SUN ☐

MY MOOD TODAY

MEDITATION

HOW LONG? _____ / _____

HOW WAS IT? HARD ☐ EASY ☐

EXCERCISE ☐

YOGA/WALKING/GYM/OTHER:
_____

✸ TODAY I CHOOSE TO FEEL
_____
_____
_____

⌖ TODAY I WILL FOCUS ON
_____
_____
_____

⚡ TODAY I FEEL INSPIRED BY
_____
_____
_____

🎲 GOOD HABITS OF THE DAY
_____
_____
_____

TO DO LIST 📝
☐ _____
☐ _____
☐ _____
☐ _____
☐ _____

TODAY I'M GRATEFUL FOR

MINDFULNESS DAILY JOURNAL

MY DAY

10 MINUTES TO REFLECT ON YOUR DAY

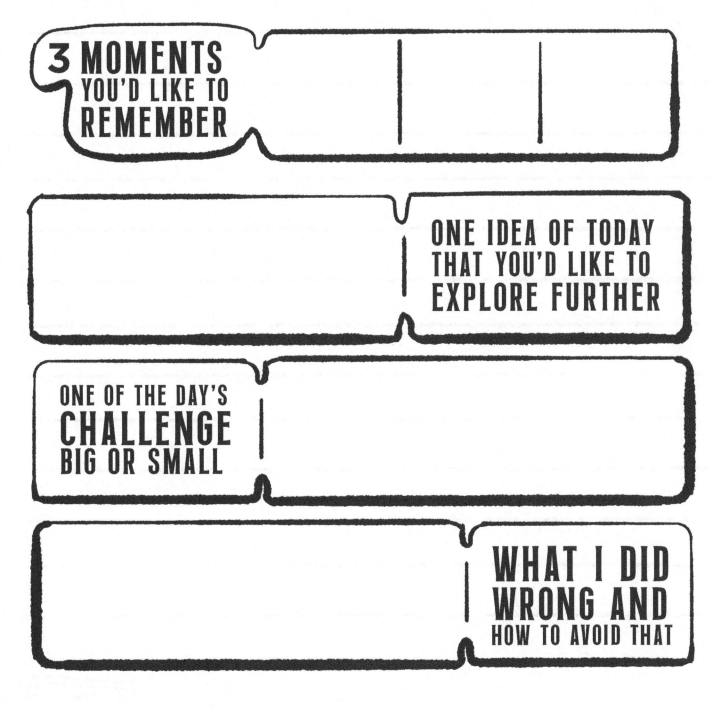

3 MOMENTS YOU'D LIKE TO REMEMBER

ONE IDEA OF TODAY THAT YOU'D LIKE TO EXPLORE FURTHER

ONE OF THE DAY'S CHALLENGE BIG OR SMALL

WHAT I DID WRONG AND HOW TO AVOID THAT

MINDFULNESS DAILY JOURNAL

JOURNAL

WOW

MINDFULNESS DAILY JOURNAL

MON ☐	TUE ☐	WED ☐

DATE: ____/____/20____

THU ☐	FRI ☐	SAT ☐	SUN ☐

MY MOOD TODAY

MEDITATION

HOW LONG? ____/____

HOW WAS IT? HARD ☐ EASY ☐

EXCERCISE ☐

YOGA/WALKING/GYM/OTHER: _____

✦ TODAY I CHOOSE TO FEEL
_____
_____
_____

◎ TODAY I WILL FOCUS ON
_____
_____
_____

⚡ TODAY I FEEL INSPIRED BY
_____
_____
_____

🎲 GOOD HABITS OF THE DAY
_____
_____
_____

TO DO LIST
☐ _____
☐ _____
☐ _____
☐ _____
☐ _____

TODAY I'M GRATEFUL FOR

MINDFULNESS DAILY JOURNAL

MY DAY

10 MINUTES TO REFLECT ON YOUR DAY

3 MOMENTS YOU'D LIKE TO REMEMBER

ONE IDEA OF TODAY THAT YOU'D LIKE TO EXPLORE FURTHER

ONE OF THE DAY'S CHALLENGE BIG OR SMALL

WHAT I DID WRONG AND HOW TO AVOID THAT

MINDFULNESS DAILY JOURNAL

JOURNAL

_____

_____

_____

_____

_____

_____

_____

_____

_____

_____

_____

_____

_____

WOW

MINDFULNESS DAILY JOURNAL

MON ☐	TUE ☐	WED ☐

DATE: _____/_____/20___

THU ☐	FRI ☐	SAT ☐	SUN ☐

MY MOOD TODAY

MEDITATION

HOW LONG? ___/___

HOW WAS IT? HARD ☐ EASY ☐

EXCERCISE ☐

YOGA/WALKING/GYM/OTHER:
_____

✦ TODAY I CHOOSE TO FEEL
_____
_____
_____

◉ TODAY I WILL FOCUS ON
_____
_____
_____

⚡ TODAY I FEEL INSPIRED BY
_____
_____
_____

🎲 GOOD HABITS OF THE DAY
_____
_____
_____

TO DO LIST
- ☐ _____
- ☐ _____
- ☐ _____
- ☐ _____
- ☐ _____

TODAY I'M GRATEFUL FOR

MINDFULNESS DAILY JOURNAL

MY DAY

10 MINUTES TO REFLECT ON YOUR DAY

3 MOMENTS YOU'D LIKE TO REMEMBER

ONE IDEA OF TODAY THAT YOU'D LIKE TO EXPLORE FURTHER

ONE OF THE DAY'S CHALLENGE BIG OR SMALL

WHAT I DID WRONG AND HOW TO AVOID THAT

MINDFULNESS DAILY JOURNAL

JOURNAL

_____

_____

_____

_____

_____

_____

_____

_____

_____

_____

_____

_____

_____

WOW

MINDFULNESS DAILY JOURNAL

MON ☐   **TUE** ☐   **WED** ☐

DATE: ____/____/20____

THU ☐   **FRI** ☐   **SAT** ☐   **SUN** ☐

MY MOOD TODAY

MEDITATION

HOW LONG? ____/____

HOW WAS IT?   HARD ☐   EASY ☐

EXCERCISE ☐

YOGA/WALKING/GYM/OTHER:
_____

✸ TODAY I CHOOSE TO FEEL
_____
_____
_____

⊙ TODAY I WILL FOCUS ON
_____
_____
_____

⚡ TODAY I FEEL INSPIRED BY
_____
_____
_____

⚅ GOOD HABITS OF THE DAY
_____
_____
_____

TO DO LIST
☐ _____
☐ _____
☐ _____
☐ _____
☐ _____

TODAY I'M GRATEFUL FOR

MINDFULNESS DAILY JOURNAL

MY DAY

10 MINUTES TO REFLECT ON YOUR DAY

3 MOMENTS YOU'D LIKE TO REMEMBER

ONE IDEA OF TODAY THAT YOU'D LIKE TO EXPLORE FURTHER

ONE OF THE DAY'S CHALLENGE BIG OR SMALL

WHAT I DID WRONG AND HOW TO AVOID THAT

MINDFULNESS DAILY JOURNAL

JOURNAL

_____

_____

_____

_____

_____

_____

_____

_____

_____

_____

_____

_____

_____

WOW